D0907401

THE 10

Strangest Mysteries

Judy Coghill

Series Editor
Jeffrey D. Wilhelm

Marion Carnegie Library
206 S. Market St.
Marion, IL 62959

Much thought, debate, and research went into choosing and ranking the 10 items in each book in this series. We realize that everyone has his or her own opinion of what is most significant, revolutionary, amazing, deadly, and so on. As you read, you may agree with our choices, or you may be surprised — and that's the way it should be!

Franklin Watts®

an imprint of

◼SCHOLASTIC

www.scholastic.com/librarypublishing

A Rubicon book published in association with Scholastic Inc.

Ru´bĭcon © 2007 Rubicon Publishing Inc.
www.rubiconpublishing.com

All rights reserved. No part of this publication may be reproduced, stored in a database or retrieval system, distributed, or transmitted in any form or by any means, electronic, mechanical, photocopying, recording, or otherwise, without the prior written permission of Rubicon Publishing Inc.

 is a trademark of The 10 Books

SCHOLASTIC and associated logos and designs are trademarks and/or registered trademarks of Scholastic Inc.

Associate Publishers: Kim Koh, Miriam Bardswich
Project Editor: Amy Land
Editor: Bettina Fehrenbach
Creative Director: Jennifer Drew
Project Manager/Designer: Jeanette MacLean
Graphic Designer: Waseem Bashar

The publisher gratefully acknowledges the following for permission to reprint copyrighted material in this book.

Every reasonable effort has been made to trace the owners of copyrighted material and to make due acknowledgment. Any errors or omissions drawn to our attention will be gladly rectified in future editions.

"Skyjacker at large; A Florida widow thinks she has found him" (excerpt), by Douglas Pasternak. From *U.S. News & World Report*, July 24, 2000. Copyright 2000 *U.S. News & World Report*, L.P. Reprinted with permission.

"Diary a clue to Amelia Earhart Mystery" (excerpt), by Richard Pyle. From *Associated Press*, April 1, 2007. Reprinted with permission.

"Bigfoot Video makes Big Dollars in U.S." (excerpt), by Dawn Walton. From *The Globe and Mail*, May 3, 2005. Reprinted with permission from *The Globe and Mail*.

Cover image: Getty Images/Stone/George Diebold Photography

Library and Archives Canada Cataloguing in Publication

Coghill, Judy, 1948-
    The 10 strangest mysteries/Judy Coghill.

Includes index.
ISBN 978-1-55448-466-9

    1. Readers (Elementary) 2. Readers—Curiosities and wonders.
I. Title. II. Title: Ten strangest mysteries.

PE1117.C626 2007   428.6   C2007-900554-3

1 2 3 4 5 6 7 8 9 10   10   16 15 14 13 12 11 10 09 08 07

Printed in Singapore

Contents

Introduction: Believe It or Not 4

The Disappearance of D.B. Cooper 6
A skyjacker who has disappeared … could he still be alive?

Lost Dutchman Mine 10
Is this gold mine cursed? You might just go crazy trying to find out.

Spontaneous Human Combustion 14
At any time and in any place a person could burn to ashes … could that be you?

Mothman 18
Hundreds of people claim to have seen this creepy creature, but does it really exist?

Where Is Amelia Earhart? 22
The disappearance of this famous aviator still has people scratching their heads!

Mary Celeste 26
An abandoned ship left in perfect condition … what could have happened to the crew?

Bigfoot 30
There could be an entire population of these creatures … if only we could actually see them.

Crop Circles 34
Are these mysterious formations created by aliens? You decide.

Elvis Presley 38
Did the King of Rock and Roll fake his death? There must be some truth to all the Elvis sightings (and we aren't talking about impersonators).

Bermuda Triangle 42
Planning to fly or sail to Bermuda? You might want to think again …

We Thought … 46

What Do You Think? 47

Index 48

14

30

34

BELIEVE IT OR NOT...

Everybody loves a good mystery, whether it's an unsolved crime or a weird happening. That's just human nature. We are naturally curious, and we want all things explained in ways that make perfect sense — what really happened and why, who or what was behind it, and what was the result? But not all things can be explained …

The strangest mysteries are the ones that remain unsolved for a long time. They confound people, and many even spend a lot of time and money trying to get at the answers. These mysteries continue to haunt and puzzle curious minds — as can be seen in the many Web sites on the subjects.

In this book, we present what we think are the 10 most puzzling mysteries. They still leave many people — even experts —baffled! In ranking them, we used these criteria: how strange are the circumstances; how many times has the mystery occurred; for how long has it been going on; what has been its impact on life and property?

As you read the selections, think like a detective and ask yourself:

confound: *mix up or confuse*

ALL IMAGES—SHUTTERSTOCK

WHAT IS THE STRANGEST MYSTERY?

This is a re-enactment of

GES—STOCKPHOTO AND SHUTTERSTOCK

ANCE OF D.B. COOPER

WHEN: November 24, 1971

WHERE: In an airplane headed from Portland, Oregon to Seattle, Washington and then to Mexico

SOMETHING STRANGE ... This clever crook was last seen jumping out of a plane one cold and stormy night. No one has a clue where he went. This is the only unsolved skyjacking in U.S. history!

On the night of November 24, 1971, a man dressed in a business suit bought a one-way ticket to Seattle at Portland International Airport in Oregon. He called himself Dan Cooper, and he paid $20 cash for the 30-minute flight. Shortly after the plane took off, Cooper handed a note to the young flight attendant. She assumed it was his phone number and stuck the note in her pocket without reading it. Only when Cooper said that she had better read it because he had a bomb, did she look at the paper and give the note to the pilot.

The note said that Cooper would blow up the plane unless the airline delivered $200,000 and two sets of parachutes to him when the plane landed in Seattle. The pilot contacted the airline. Officials had 20 minutes to meet Cooper's demands. As the plane circled the airport at Seattle, waiting for Cooper's demands to be met, only a few passengers were aware of the real problem.

THE PLOT THICKENS

This was a very well-planned crime. With an airplane full of passengers, Cooper asked for $200,000 in $20 bills in exchange for their safe release. The airline could not risk the lives of the passengers. It had no choice but to give Cooper what he wanted. Once his demands were met, Cooper allowed the passengers to leave the plane but kept the flight crew onboard. The crew was told to take off again toward Mexico. About 25 miles north of Portland, Cooper jumped out of the plane. He has never been seen again.

? Do you think a crime like Cooper's could happen today? Why or why not?

THEORY #1

Cooper was wearing a suit, an overcoat, and loafers. He parachuted from a height of more than 9,800 feet in the air, and plunged into the darkness of a late November storm with a wind chill temperature of -69°F. His loafers would have been blown off his feet almost immediately. But it is possible he could have survived 15 seconds of this cold temperature until he landed. Cooper might have instructed someone to be waiting on the ground to help him make a quick escape.

THEORY #2

Cooper died. The parachute could have failed. He could have landed in the river and drowned in the icy waters. Or, without warm clothing, shoes, and food, he may not have been able to get out of the snow-filled forest alive.

? Assume that Cooper survived the jump. How do you think he could have avoided getting caught?

This is a composite sketch of D.B. Cooper, drawn by FBI officials.

Quick Fact

Cooper thought he was being clever by asking for $20 bills with random serial numbers (so they couldn't be traced to him). The FBI did this, but they used a high-speed photocopier to copy each of the bills so the serial numbers could be traced later.

The Expert Says...

It was an extraordinary, audacious act to lower that rear gangway in flight and jump into a dark and stormy night.

— Walt Crowley, historian

audacious: *daring*

Skyjacker at large
A Florida widow thinks she has found him

An article from *U.S. News & World Report*
By Douglas Pasternak, July 24, 2000

In March 1995, a Florida antique dealer named Duane Weber lay dying … in a hospital. He called his wife, Jo, to his bed and whispered: "I'm Dan Cooper." Jo, who had learned in 17 years of marriage not to pry too deeply into Duane's past, had no idea what her secretive husband meant. Frustrated, he blurted out: "Oh, let it die with me!" Duane died 11 days later. …

In May 1996, Jo checked out a library book on D.B. Cooper. "I did not realize D.B. Cooper was known as Dan Cooper," Jo says. The book listed the FBI's description: mid-40s, six feet tall, 170 pounds, black hair, a bourbon drinker, a chain-smoker. At the time of the hijacking, Duane Weber was 47, six feet, one inch tall, and weighed around 185 pounds. He had black hair, drank bourbon, and chain-smoked.

The similarities between a younger Duane and the FBI's composite drawings struck Jo. "It's about as close a match as you can get," agrees Frank Bender … who has worked with the FBI for 20 years. …

Jo called the FBI the night she read the D.B. Cooper book. "They just blew me off," she says. Eventually she began a dialogue with Ralph Himmelsbach, the FBI agent in charge of the case from 1971 until his retirement in 1980. At his urging, the FBI opened a file on Duane Weber in March 1997. … Himmelsbach finds Jo Weber, who has agreed to take a polygraph test, to be credible. There is no reward money to motivate her. He thinks she simply wants to learn the truth about her spouse. "The facts she has really seem to fit," he says. But the FBI dropped its investigation of Weber in July 1998. More "conclusive evidence" would be needed to continue, they say. …

A BULLETIN FROM THE F.B.I.

Following is an artist's conception of the hijacker who extorted $200,000 from Northwest Airlines on November 24, 1971.

THIS MAN IS DESCRIBED AS FOLLOWS:

Race	White
Sex	Male
Age	Mid 40's
Height	5' 10" to 6'
Weight	170 to 180 pounds
Build	Average to well built
Complexion	Olive, Latin appearance, medium smooth
Hair	Dark brown or black, normal style, parted on left, combed back; sideburns, low ear level
Eyes	Possibly brown. During latter part of flight put on dark, wrap-around sunglasses with dark rims
Voice	Low, spoke intelligently; no particular accent, possibly from Midwest section of U.S.
Characteristics	Heavy smoker of Raleigh filter tip cigarettes
Wearing Apparel	Black suit; white shirt; narrow black tie; black dress suit; black rain-type overcoat or dark top coat; dark briefcase or attache case; carried paper bag 4" x 12" x 14"; brown shoes.

If you have any information which might lead to the identity of this individual, please contact the nearest FBI Office which would be found in the front of your telephone directory.

Quick Fact

After this skyjacking, the U.S. Federal Aviation Association (FAA) required all Boeing 727s to be fitted with a mechanical wedge that locks the plane's door from the outside while in flight. This device is nicknamed the "Cooper Vane."

Take Note

This crime stands at #10 on our list of strangest mysteries because more than 30 years after it happened, no one knows what really happened to D.B. Cooper.
• What do you think happened to Cooper? Keep in mind that his body and the money he stole were never found.

⑨ LOST DUTCHM

Superstition Mountain

MYSTERIOUS MINES—ISTOCKPHOTO

AN MINE

WHEN: Late 19th century

WHEN: Late 19th century

WHERE: Superstition Mountain near Phoenix, Arizona

SOMETHING STRANGE ... Hundreds of treasure-seekers have just disappeared, gone mad, or died mysteriously while trying to find the amazing treasures of the Lost Dutchman Mine.

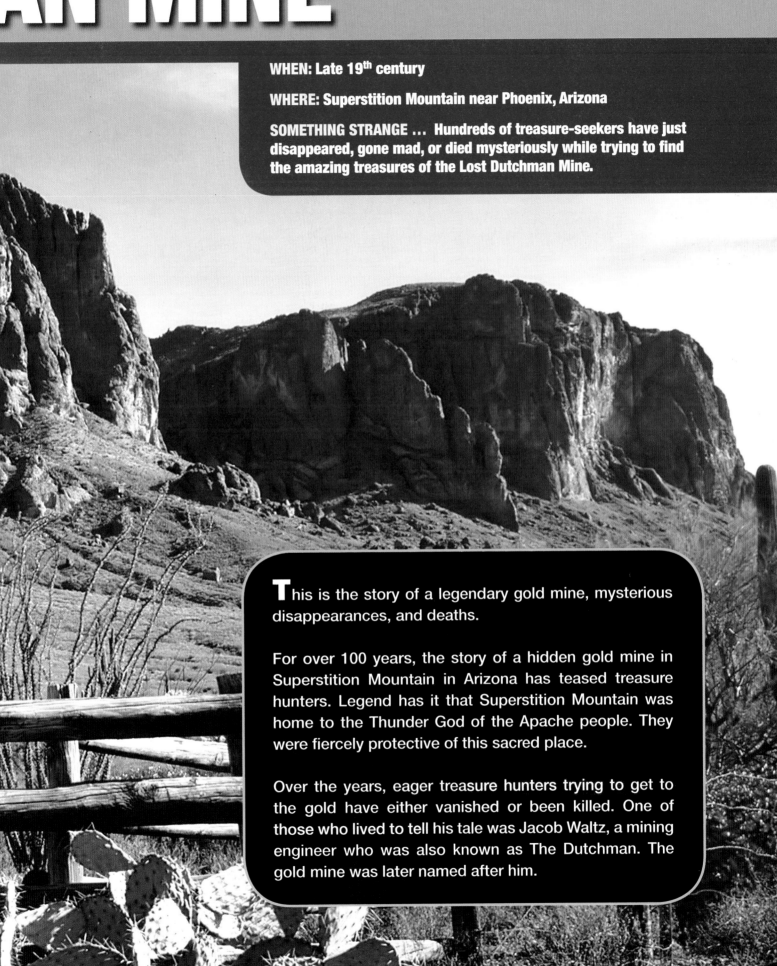

This is the story of a legendary gold mine, mysterious disappearances, and deaths.

For over 100 years, the story of a hidden gold mine in Superstition Mountain in Arizona has teased treasure hunters. Legend has it that Superstition Mountain was home to the Thunder God of the Apache people. They were fiercely protective of this sacred place.

Over the years, eager treasure hunters trying to get to the gold have either vanished or been killed. One of those who lived to tell his tale was Jacob Waltz, a mining engineer who was also known as The Dutchman. The gold mine was later named after him.

LOST DUTCHMAN MINE

Coal miners get ready to enter the Lost Dutchman Mine.

THE PLOT THICKENS

In the 16th century, Francisco Vasquez de Coronado, a Spanish conqueror, went in search of the mine. His men disappeared and Coronado named the mountain Superstition Mountain. Three hundred years later, Don Miguel Peralta, a Mexican landowner, discovered the gold mine in 1845. The first written record of gold being found in Superstition Mountain is dated 1864 when six prospectors discovered a ledge of gold ore. A few years later, Jacob Waltz also went there in search of gold. Waltz claimed to have found a rich mine full of gold but he took the details of the secret location to the grave with him.

THEORY #1

Waltz never actually made it to the mine because it was fiercely guarded by the Apaches. The Apaches were most likely the first people to find the mountain and discover its riches. They didn't take the gold for themselves because they were afraid of the Thunder God who was said to live there and protect the gold. Because of this, superstitions about the mountain surfaced.

prospectors: *people searching for gold and minerals*

THEORY #2

Waltz obtained a map to the mine from one of Peralta's descendants. Waltz and his partner, Jacob Weiser, located the mine and mined for gold together. Weiser may have been killed by Waltz. Other people who disappeared may have been killed by the Apache people who were protecting their sacred site. For some reason, Waltz closed up the mine and never returned to it. Before his death, he told his neighbor about the mine, but she never found it.

Why do gold and money make people greedy? Do you think you would ever become this way?

Quick Fact

What's in a nickname? For some unknown reason, Jacob Waltz became known as "the Dutchman" even though he was born in Germany!

This is an abandoned house just outside the mines.

The Expert Says...

"The Lost Dutchman Mine has fired the imaginations of men and women for more than a century. Just maybe it is not so much the finding as it is the searching."

— Tom Kollenborn, Superstition Mountain Historical Society

MINERS—ZUMA PRESS/KEYSTONE PRESS; OTHER IMAGES—SHUTTERSTOCK, ISTOCKPHOTO

RAIDERS OF THE LOST GOLD

People have been talking about this gold mine for over 400 years, so why hasn't anyone made the BIG discovery? Perhaps it's because not every treasure hunter who visits Superstition Mountain makes it back alive. So what's the deal? Is the gold cursed? Are the Apaches still guarding it? Read this timeline and decide for yourself.

MUTILATION MOUNTAIN

1540: Francisco Vasquez de Coronado and his men are told of the gold by the Apaches. But when they go in search of the gold, men begin disappearing and are later found, mutilated. Coronado names the mountain *Monte Superstition*, or Superstition Mountain.

PERALTA MASSACRE

1845: A Mexican named Don Miguel Peralta finds the mine and goes with his men to retrieve the gold and bring it back to Mexico. Legend has it that the Apaches discover this plan and kill them all.

THE LYING DUTCHMAN?

1860s: Jacob Waltz (aka the Dutchman) goes in search of the gold. He claims he found the mine, but no one ever knows the truth. He dies with a few gold nuggets under his bed.

PRESCRIPTION FOR RICHES

1870: Dr. Abraham Thorne befriends the Apaches by being their physician for many years. One day they blindfold him and lead him to the mine. He finds the gold. He takes as much as he can and sells it for thousands of dollars.

> Legend states that the Apaches kill any trespassers who come to the mountain, yet they took Dr. Thorne to the mine to take gold. Why do you think the Apaches helped the doctor find the gold if they didn't allow others to find it?

DEAD MEN TELL NO TALES

1947: In his search for the gold, retired photographer James A. Cravey has a helicopter drop him off near Superstition Mountain. Two weeks later, the pilot returns to the meeting place to pick up Cravey, but he is nowhere to be seen. A few months later his headless skeleton is found.

Quick Fact

He's a determined gold digger! Former Arizona Attorney General Bob Corbin strongly believes there is gold hidden in Superstition Mountain. That's why he's visited it hundreds of times in the last 50 years.

Take Note

The Lost Dutchman Mine stands at #9 on our list. Its mystery isn't likely to be solved anytime soon — the people who claimed to have been there are long dead. However, prospectors are still searching for the lost mine.
• Would you want gold that could be cursed? Why or why not?

5   4   3   2   1

Over the last 300 years, at least 200 cases of SHC have been reported.

HEAD BURSTING WITH FLAMES-GETTY IMAGES/PHOTOGRAPHER'S CHOICE/ADRI BERGER/200151608-001

MAN COMBUSTION

WHEN: It could happen anytime

WHERE: Usually when a person is alone in his or her home

SOMETHING STRANGE … People turning into fireballs for no visible reason. You won't think the Human Torch is just a comic book character after reading about this gruesome mystery.

Imagine a fire so hot that it can turn a human body into a pile of bones and ashes. And if that's not mysterious enough, at the scene there are no visible causes for the fire, and nothing else in the room is damaged.

This is not a new phenomenon. It is called spontaneous human combustion or SHC. Some people claim the first real documented case of SHC was in the 1800s. Then there's the FBI and the scientists who claim that it doesn't exist at all.

In the 1800s, it was thought that a bad diet or too much liquor caused SHC. Some people are still convinced that SHC is the work of mysterious supernatural forces.

So … has this sparked your interest in spontaneous human combustion? Put on your flame-proof gloves and turn the page to find out more.

---

spontaneous: *happening without a visible cause*
combustion: *the process of burning*

THE PLOT THICKENS

The first reliable historic evidence of SHC appears to be from the year 1673, when a French writer published a collection of spontaneous human combustion case studies. He was inspired to write this book after finding records of a spooky court case. The court records told of a man who was found reduced to ashes in his straw bed, leaving just his skull and finger bones.

THEORY #1

Some people believe that spontaneous human combustion can only be explained by supernatural forces or psychic powers. It is difficult to explain why, in cases of SHC, the bones are almost completely destroyed when very little around the body is burned. Crematoriums require temperatures close to 1800°F to burn human bones.

> From what you know of fires, why is it hard to believe that a body can burn to ashes, yet nothing else is damaged?

THEORY #2

One of the possible scientific explanations for SHC is called the "wick effect." It is thought that a person falls asleep with a cigarette or near a candle and accidentally sets his or her clothes on fire. The clothes then act like the wick of the candle, and the person's body fat becomes the fuel. The fire burns on until all the fat is used up.

ALL IMAGES—SHUTTERSTOCK

Quick Fact

Poor piggy! In one experiment, Dr. John de Haan used a dead pig to demonstrate the wick effect (pigs have about the same fat content as humans). The pig was covered in a blanket and set on fire. After burning for five hours, it was revealed that the bones were destroyed in the same way as

The Expert Says...

❝ There's one mystery I'm asked about more than any other — spontaneous human combustion. Some cases seem to defy explanation and leave me with a creepy and very unscientific feeling. If there's anything more to SHC, I simply don't want to know. ❞

Hot Stuff!

Don't fully believe in spontaneous human combustion yet? Well, this list contains seven more reasons to convince you that SHC is more than a mystery!

1 On April 9, 1744, Grace Pett, 60, a woman living in Ipswich, England, was found dead. Her daughter said the body looked like "a log of wood consumed by a fire, without apparent flame." Nearby clothing was undamaged.

2 Larry Arnold, author of *Ablaze!,* is considered one of the leading SHC experts. He has collected over 400 spontaneous human combustion case studies. He says there is an increase in cases every 33 years, which could be related to cycles of high solar activity.

3 Some of the common factors in reported SHC cases: 80 percent of the victims were female, most of the victims were overweight and/or alcoholics, the victim was always alone, and the victim was drinking heavily prior to burning.

4 In 1852, author Charles Dickens used SHC to kill off Krook, a character in his novel *Bleak House*. Krook was an alcoholic, true to the popular belief at the time that SHC was caused by excessive drinking.

5 In cases of SHC, the burns are not distributed evenly over the body; the hands and feet are usually untouched by fire, whereas the torso usually suffers severe burning.

? How does this tie in to the wick theory?

6 People who were in the area of the SHC incidents reported never hearing any cries of pain or calls for assistance.

7 Mary Hardy Reeser, a 67-year-old widow, spontaneously combusted while sitting in her easy chair on July 1, 1951. Her remains were found in a blackened circle about five feet in diameter. All that was left of the 175-pound woman was a section of her backbone, a shrunken skull the size of a baseball, one foot, and 10 pounds of ashes.

Quick Fact

Could passing gas be the cause of SHC? Some people believe that methane, a flammable gas produced in our intestines, can build up to a point where enzymes cause this gas to catch fire.

enzymes: *proteins that speed up chemical reactions*

Take Note

Like the Dutchman mystery, SHC has been unsolved for a very long time. SHC ranks #8 because it actually kills people and yet there are no believable explanations.
- Of all the theories about what causes SHC, which do you find most convincing and why?

5   4   3   2   1

This is an illustration of *Mothman* by Cathy Wilkins.

MOTHMAN ILLUSTRATION–CATHY WILKINS

WHEN: November 1966 to December 1967

WHERE: Point Pleasant, West Virginia

SOMETHING STRANGE … This flying monster with glowing red eyes terrified the people of Point Pleasant for over a year. Could hundreds of citizens have imagined the same thing?

It may be named after a character from the 1960s *Batman* TV series, but that didn't stop Mothman from striking fear into the hearts of all kinds of people. Imagine you are driving down a dark road late at night. Suddenly you see a human-sized creature with a 10-foot wingspan. As you try to speed away, the creature hovers over you staring with its huge glowing red eyes.

This type of spooky sighting would be easy to dismiss as someone's mind playing tricks — if it had happened once or twice. But over a period of 13 months, more than 100 people in the Point Pleasant area reported experiences like this. In the words of eyewitness Linda Scarberry, "It was those eyes that got us. It had two big red eyes, like automobile reflectors."

So … is it a bird? Or perhaps the bizarre result of a government toxic waste experiment gone wrong? There are several theories about Mothman … which will you believe?

MOTHMAN

THE PLOT THICKENS

Mothman got its name from its appearance. The coloring of its body and wings made it look like a giant moth. Mothman's appearances were linked with strange occurrences: static interference on TVs, radios, and telephones; pets and farm animals found mutilated; and strange notes sent to families warning of an approaching disaster. On December 15, 1967, Point Pleasant's Silver Bridge collapsed, killing 46 people. Right after this, the Mothman sightings stopped. Some people believe the collapse of the bridge was what the Mothman had been warning them about.

THEORY #1

This theory sounds like something out of a comic book — toxic waste, abandoned factories, and government experiments gone wrong. Mothman was often spotted around an abandoned explosives factory, so people thought it had mutated from chemicals that had been stored there since World War II. Some thought he was a bird that mutated during a secret experiment at the factory. A few people reported strangely dressed agents coming to question them about the Mothman sightings.

THEORY #2

Some people think that the Mothman was actually a large bird such as the sandhill crane. Sandhill cranes can be as tall as six feet. They have wing spans of 10 feet and can glide for long distances without flapping their wings. The glowing eyes could have been due to the reflections of car lights or other lights in the area.

? Why do supernatural events continue to fascinate us?

An 11.5-foot-tall statue of the Mothman stands in Point Pleasant.

Quick Fact

A cryptozoologist studies "hidden" animals such as Mothman, Bigfoot, and the Loch Ness Monster. These creatures have not been recognized by formal zoology, but evidence of their existence has been supported by eyewitness accounts.

zoology: *the study of classification of animals*

The Expert Says...

" In all my investigations over the years I've found that 80 percent of [Mothman sightings] are misidentifications or hoaxes, but there are some with at least a kernel of truth. What I try to do with any of these is present data, and if you present enough data, there might be some acceptance of what happened. "

— Loren Coleman, cryptozoologist, Mothman expert

ALL IMAGES-SHUTTERSTOCK

The Legend of MOTHMAN

Do you wonder how the events and sightings of Mothman unfolded between November 1966 and December 1967? The timeline below documents only a small number of the hundred sightings by people who witnessed this scary creature.

NOVEMBER 12, 1966

Five men are in a cemetery in Clendenin, West Virginia. They see something that looks like a "brown human being" lift off from some nearby trees and fly over their heads.

NOVEMBER 15, 1966

Two young married couples drive past an abandoned TNT plant near Point Pleasant. They spot two large eyes that are attached to something that is "shaped like a man, but bigger, maybe six or seven feet tall, with wings folded against its back."

NOVEMBER 21, 1966

Richard West, of Charleston, calls the police and reports a winged figure sitting on the roof of his neighbor's house. The six-foot-tall figure has a wingspan of six to eight feet and red eyes. It takes off straight up, "like a helicopter."

DECEMBER 4, 1966

Five pilots at the Gallipolis, Ohio, airport see some sort of giant bird flying at about 70 miles per hour. Its wings aren't moving, and it's gliding across the sky.

JANUARY 11, 1967

Mabel McDaniel (mother of Linda Scarberry, another witness) sees Mothman. She says the creature looks like "an airplane." [T]hen I realized it was flying much too low. It was brown and had a wingspan of at least 10 feet."

DECEMBER 15, 1967

The 700-foot bridge linking Point Pleasant to Ohio suddenly collapses while filled with rush-hour traffic. Dozens of vehicles plunge into the dark waters of the Ohio River. Forty-six people are killed.

"I wish we had never seen it, I wish someone else had seen i[t]

—Linda Scarberry, eyewitness, November 15, 1[9...]

Quick Fact

Some say that the Mothman sightings of 1966–67 were just a case of mass hysteria. This phenomenon usually starts with one person who believes strongly in a fake idea. The idea then spreads quickly and "contagiously" to several people. The details usually become more frightening as the story travels.

hysteria: *uncontrollable emotion*

Take Note

Like several of the previous mysteries, this is intriguing. Mothman is an unusual creature who has had many sightings by credible sources. Yet, there is no simple or logical explanation for the creature's numerous appearances in this small area. Mothman flies into the #7 spot.

- Use a dictionary to look up the words "supernatural" and "paranormal." In your own words describe the difference between the two.

On May 20, 1932, Earhart became the second person to fly solo across the Atlantic Ocean. (Charles Lindbergh was the first.)

ELIA EARHART?

WHEN: July 2, 1937

WHERE: In the Pacific Ocean — somewhere between Lae, New Guinea and Howland Island

SOMETHING STRANGE ... The biggest air and sea rescue of that time occurred, but Earhart, her plane, and her navigator were never found!

Setting a world record is quite an achievement. Your name is in the paper, you become a celebrity, and you've accomplished something no one has ever done before. Amelia Earhart wanted to be the first woman to fly around the world. She had already set numerous records as a female aviator: reaching the highest altitude; flying solo across the Atlantic Ocean; and flying solo from Mexico City to Newark, New Jersey, among others.

For several weeks the world focused on this fearless flier who dared to be the first woman to fly around the world. She had almost completed her 29,000-mile flight when tragedy struck. Earhart, her navigator Fred Noonan, and her plane disappeared.

In the years since, various stories have surfaced as to what happened to Earhart. The most believable story is that her plane ran out of gas on her way to Howland Island, and she crashed into the Pacific Ocean. Even though there were several ships stationed along her flight route, no trace of the plane or the bodies of Earhart and Noonan has ever been found. So the question remains: What on Earth happened to Amelia Earhart?

THE PLOT THICKENS

On June 1, 1937, Earhart and Noonan departed Miami, Florida. On June 29, they landed in Lae, New Guinea, with only 7,000 miles left to go. Their next stop was Howland Island, a tiny island 2,556 miles from Lae in the mid-Pacific. The U.S. Coast Guard ship *Itasca* was stationed just offshore. Three other U.S. ships were positioned along Earhart's flight path as markers. Earhart and Noonan left Lae at 12:30 AM and flew into an overcast and rainy sky. Despite several attempts to contact and locate Earhart, the *Itasca* could not identify her location.

What do you think the mood was aboard the *Itasca* as they waited to hear word from Earhart?

Earhart once said of dying, "When I go, I'd like best to go in my plane."

THEORY #1

Earhart's flight took place two years before the outbreak of World War II. The U.S. believed that Japan was taking control of many islands in the Pacific Ocean and secretly preparing for war. U.S. President Franklin D. Roosevelt took advantage of Earhart's flight over that area and asked that she spy on the Japanese and report her findings to him. The Japanese were onto Earhart's plan, and either shot down her plane and captured her or she died as her plane crashed into the ocean.

THEORY #2

Because of bad weather and unclear transmissions, Noonan had a hard time identifying their position. Earhart and Noonan were most likely off course and the plane ran out of gas. The plane plunged into the Pacific Ocean and sank to the bottom of the ocean. Because the U.S. ships were unaware of Earhart's off-course location, the Navy was searching hundreds of miles from where her plane actually crashed.

Quick Fact

In 1938, a corked bottle with a message in it washed up on the coast of France. The message said that the writer was a prisoner in the South Pacific where Earhart and a man were being held prisoner by the Japanese for spying.

Quick Fact

The United States government spent $4 million looking for Earhart, which made it the most costly and intensive air and sea search in history at that time.

Why do you think the government spent so much?

AMELIA EARHART–ZUMA PRESS/KEYSTONE PRESS;

Diary a Clue to Amelia Earhart Mystery

**An article from Associated Press,
By Richard Pyle, April 1, 2007**

… Also listening in the *Itasca's* radio room was James W. Carey, one of two reporters aboard. The 23-year-old University of Hawaii student had been hired by the Associated Press [AP] to cover Earhart's Howland stopover. His job was to send brief radiograms to the AP in Honolulu and San Francisco.

But during the eight days since arriving at Howland, Carey also had been keeping a diary. …

Carey's diary was unknown to Earhart scholars until last September, when a typewritten copy turned up on eBay and was bought by a member of The International Group for Historic Aircraft Recovery, or TIGHAR. The non-profit organization believes Earhart and Noonan were not lost at sea, but landed on an uninhabited atoll called Gardner Island, and lived for an unknown period as castaways.

"Even though the diary doesn't answer the big question, it's an incredible discovery," said TIGHAR executive director Ric Gillespie, who has led eight expeditions to the island since 1989, and plans another this July if his group can raise enough money. …

Seventy years later, the mystery lingers. Millions have been spent on expeditions and deep-sea probes, and although legally declared dead by a California court in early 1939, Earhart has been the subject of more than 50 nonfiction books.

Now raising funds for a ninth TIGHAR expedition to Nikumaroro in July, Gillespie says the Carey diary serves as a reminder to always "expect the unexpected" in the Earhart case. …

---

atoll: *coral island consisting of a reef surrounding a shallow pond*

The Expert Says…

" While logically we know she [Earhart] is dead, those who consign her to myth feel she is still alive, and know she is incapable of such a simple fate as getting lost. "

— Henry M. Holden, author of *The Mystery Lingers On: Amelia Earhart*

consign: *give over to*

Take Note

Seventy years after Amelia Earhart's disappearance, people are still determined to solve the mystery. Millions of people knew about Earhart and her plan to fly around the world, and millions of people still wonder what happened to this famous aviator. Amelia Earhart's disappearance ranks #6 on our list.

• Why do you think people risk their lives to be the first to do something and set records? Are you willing to risk your life to make headlines? Explain your answers.

5 MARY CELESTE

Although no picture of the Mary Celeste is known to exist, many believe it might have looked like this ship from the same period.

TALL SHIP WITH FULL SAILS–GETTY IMAGES/STONE/REX ZIAK/AR5809–001

WHEN: December 4, 1872

WHERE: Atlantic Ocean, 500 miles west of Spain

SOMETHING STRANGE ... The legend of the *Mary Celeste* ghost ship is a haunting reminder of the mysterious powers of the sea.

Imagine being out in the middle of the Atlantic Ocean and coming across a 100-foot-long ship with no one onboard. You and your crew are curious (and a little afraid), but decide to check it out. The ship is in almost perfect condition — it hasn't been through a storm, and it definitely hasn't been robbed. There is even a cat sleeping peacefully in one of the rooms! So what gives?

In the days of the *Mary Celeste*, ships did not have the technology that they have today. Horrible storms or rocky cliffs were a common threat, and many ships disappeared, never to be seen again. The story of the *Mary Celeste* is so mysterious because the ship was left intact, but the crew had disappeared without a trace.

It couldn't have been a pirate attack because the ship's money box and cargo were untouched. Other explanations ranged from a giant squid pulling people off the ship, tidal waves throwing everyone into the sea, and even alien abductions!

MARY CELESTE

Captain Benjamin Briggs

THE PLOT THICKENS

The *Mary Celeste* was 100 feet long and weighed 280 tons. In 1872, it came under the command of Captain Benjamin Briggs, who was known as an excellent sailor. He set sail for Genoa, Italy, with his wife, daughter, and a crew of seven on November 7. Twenty-seven days later, the *Mary Celeste* was found abandoned and drifting in the Atlantic Ocean. The *Mary Celeste* was first spotted by Captain David Reed Morehouse, the captain of the *Dei Gratia*. He and his crew found no one onboard. The last entry in the ship's log was on November 24.

THEORY #1

The *Mary Celeste* was carrying a cargo of industrial alcohol. When the ship was found, a few of the barrels were empty. Some people believe that the alcohol started to seep out, and the fumes became very strong. The captain feared the ship was going to explode, so he ordered the crew into a lifeboat. Although the lifeboat was tied to the ship, a gust of wind caused the *Mary Celeste* to pick up speed. The rope broke, and the crew was lost at sea.

THEORY #2

One theory suggests that Captain Morehouse, who found the *Mary Celeste*, killed everyone onboard and later claimed to have found the ship abandoned. This way Morehouse could keep the insurance money for himself, and no one would ever know.

Which of these two theories do you think is closer to the truth?

The Expert Says...

" Nobody seems to have had any luck with that ship at all. ... It looks like the jinx of the *Mary Celeste* has continued into the 21st century, and she is getting the last laugh from the grave. "

— Paul Begg, author of *Mary Celeste: The Great Mystery of the Sea*

Quick Fact

A year after the *Mary Celeste* was found drifting, two lifeboats with six bodies and an American flag were found on the beach at Gibraltar. The bodies were never identified. Three of the *Mary Celeste's* crew members were American.

ALL IMAGES—SHUTTERSTOCK

BLOODY MARY

The *Mary Celeste* is definitely cursed with a serious case of bad luck — just look at the numbers in this fact chart.

1861 The year that the *Amazon* (later named *Mary Celeste*) was first launched in Nova Scotia, Canada. Soon afterward, crew members reported seeing ghosts. The ship's first captain died before completing the maiden voyage.

48 The number of hours that the first captain was in charge of the ship before he died.

3 The number of times the *Mary Celeste* crashed into rocky coast-lines. It happened in Maine, and in Nova Scotia and Newfoundland, Canada.

1885 The year that the last captain of the *Mary Celeste* loaded it with cat food and cheap rubber boots and wrecked it on purpose to try and get the insurance money. He was caught and jailed for insurance fraud.

12 The number of years (1872 to 1884) that the *Mary Celeste* sat unused. Many sailors refused to sail on the ship because they thought it was haunted.

$3,000 The price that Captain Benjamin Briggs paid for the *Mary Celeste* at an auction in 1872. By this time the ship had been repaired several times.

12 The number of wood samples taken from a wreck found on August 9, 2001 off the coast of Haiti. The tests on the samples revealed that the ship was the *Mary Celeste*. It is not known exactly when the ship crashed.

? After reading these stories, do you think the *Mary Celeste* is cursed? Why or why not?

Take Note

The mystery of the *Mary Celeste* ranks #5 because more than 130 years after the event, no one has a clue as to what happened to the ship's crew and passengers.
- Do you agree with our ranking of the *Mary Celeste*? Give reasons for your answer.

5   4   3   2   1

4 BIGFOOT

According to one Bigfoot expert, at least 80 percent of the sightings are mistakes or hoaxes. People claim this is a photo of a real Bigfoot.

WHEN: Before the arrival of native peoples

WHERE: All over the world, but mainly along the Pacific coast of North America

SOMETHING STRANGE ... A tall, hairy, ape-like creature living among us? Many claim to have seen it, but where's the proof?

In isolated areas of North America, people claim to have seen a strange creature. "Bigfoot" is said to be between 6.5 and 10 feet tall and weigh between 650 and 900 pounds. Bigfoot is covered with dark brown or reddish hair and has enormous feet.

Newspapers began reporting the sightings of Bigfoot during the 1920s. Between 2,000 and 6,000 of these creatures are believed to be living in Canadian and Californian forests. People are so interested in finding Bigfoot that they have set up research centers and have come from around the world to find it. Some local authorities protect the creature. They make it illegal to kill Bigfoot! The fine is $1,000 and five years in jail.

Bigfoot is believed to be harmless. There are only a few reports of Bigfoot chasing people or raiding campsites for food.

Bigfoot is always on the run. This explains why it is difficult to get a clear picture of this strange creature.

So ... is Bigfoot real or imaginary?

BIGFOOT IN FOREST–GETTY IMAGES/PHOTONICA/3701-003824

BIGFOOT

THE PLOT THICKENS

Bigfoot lives near water in remote areas. It feeds on vegetation, including nuts and berries. It also eats fish or animals such as deer. Thousands of sightings have been reported, mainly in the last 100 years. There is a possibility that Bigfoot has lived in North America longer than native peoples. In fact, some native peoples believe Bigfoot exists. They call it Sasquatch, which means "hairy giant."

> **?** What would you do if you were alone and spotted Bigfoot? How would you prove to the public you were telling the truth?

THEORY #1

There have been sightings of Bigfoot. In October 1967, Roger Patterson and Bob Gimlin shot a 16-mm film of Bigfoot in northern California. Bigfoot was seen on film walking away from the men. Some experts who examined the Patterson tape thought they were true. In 1967, it was harder to create a hoax on film. Also, as recently as 2005, further video footage of Bigfoot was made. In addition to Bigfoot sightings, people reported finding traces of hair and footprints.

Quick Fact

The Bigfoot Researchers Field Organization (BRFO) has been set up to provide information about Bigfoot. Its aim is to resolve the Bigfoot mystery.

Quick Fact

Yeti, or the Abominable Snowman, is a creature similar to Bigfoot. People claim to have seen it in the Himalaya region of Asia.

THEORY #2

Some people claim Patterson's film is a hoax. They think Bigfoot is actually a person wearing an ape costume and making fake footprints. As well, it's hard to believe that with so many people looking for Bigfoot, so few are actually seeing it and photographing it. And if they are, where is the evidence? Many scientists argue that people who claim to have seen Bigfoot are either seeing a hoax or are creating something from nothing.

> **?** Based on the information you have read, do you think Bigfoot exists? Write down all the arguments under two lists: Fact and Fiction. After the lists are completed, make your own decision. What did you choose and why?

Patterson and Gimlin's film of Bigfoot from 1967 was very blurry.

The Expert Says...

" The vision of such creatures stomping barefoot through the forests of northwest [North] America, unknown to science, is beyond common sense. Yet reason argues that this is the case. "

— John Napier, *Bigfoot: The Yeti and Sasquatch in Myth and Reality*

BIGFOOT VIDEO—RUE DES ARCHIVES/THE GRANGER COLLECTION, NEW YORK: OTHER IMAGES—SHUTTERSTOCK

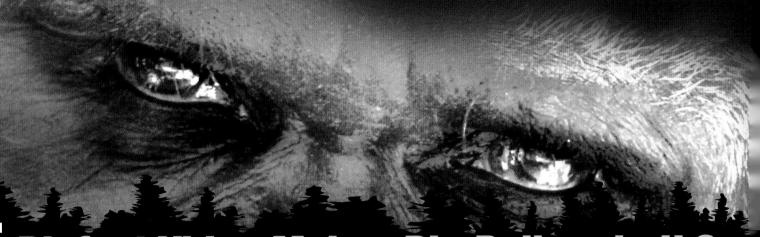

Bigfoot Video Makes Big Dollars in U.S.

An article from *The Globe and Mail*, Toronto, Canada
By Dawn Walton, May 3, 2005

CALGARY — The Canadian Sasquatch story ... complete with video of a massive, hairy beast ... will air tomorrow night on *A Current Affair* ... the Fox network said. ...

Matt Moneymaker, a Sasquatch hunter and the director of the U.S.-based Bigfoot Field Researchers Organization, has viewed the video which was shot along the Nelson River about 500 kilometres [300 miles] north of Winnipeg [Canada]. ...

"... The full circumstances of this incident point to a credible encounter," Mr. Moneymaker says on his organization's website.

He describes the image as blurry and shot from a distance, but clearly not an illusion caused by light. ... "[It is] a dark, upright, primate figure, with arms and legs somewhat like a human, standing on a riverbank," he writes.

Bobby Clarke, the videographer, ... is a ferry operator who was working an early morning shift when he spotted something peculiar on the river bank. The images, shot with a camcorder that he is rarely without, show about 30 seconds of a huge, hairy creature some viewers have described as perhaps three metres tall [almost 10 feet]. The video has been viewed by hundreds of people in Mr. Clarke's mother's living room in their remote community.

"It's a long-term thing for the family and for tourism in the community," Mr. Saunders [Mrs. Clarke's uncle and local councilman] said.

Mr. Saunders said it was important to the family to have the video assessed by an expert and they were thrilled with Mr. Moneymaker's opinion.

Quick Fact

In an unusual incident, former U.S. President Teddy Roosevelt, in his book, *The Wilderness Hunter* (1890), reported a Sasquatch stalking two trappers who had fired at it. Later, one of the trappers was found with his neck broken. There were claw and teeth marks on his neck.

Take Note

Bigfoot is #4 because it has existed as an unsolved mystery for a very long time. Like Mothman, this is a creature that many people claim to have seen. Unlike Mothman, Bigfoot seems to belong to a species and is not a single creature. Bigfoot still continues to intrigue people today.

• Would you believe someone if they told you he or she saw Bigfoot? Why or why not?

3 CROP CIRCLES

This crop circle was found in 1990 in Hampshire, England.

WHERE: Around the world, but mainly in England

WHEN: Since the 1700s

SOMETHING STRANGE ... Several bizarre symbols suddenly appear in farmers' fields. Could they be messages from space aliens?

These strange designs show up mysteriously in the middle of open fields. Crop circles, as they are called, have even appeared in fenced-in military fields, but no one has been seen making them! Scientists and researchers have spent a great deal of time trying to find out how these crop circles are created. The plants appear to be exposed to a short and intense wave of heat. Could it be a satellite sending electromagnetic waves of heat to the Earth, as some people believe?

After M. Night Shyamalan's movie, *Signs,* was released in August 2002, the public has become more fascinated than ever with crop circles. Actor Mel Gibson thinks the circles cannot simply be explained by human actions alone. He is quick to add that it doesn't mean he believes in aliens!

Some people who visit crop circles experience a heightened awareness or a sense of healing. Others feel nauseous or dizzy. There are times when electronic equipment, watches, and radios stop working.

So ... how do these mysterious circles keep popping up?

CROP CIRCLES

THE PLOT THICKENS

Large, geometrical, flattened areas have been appearing in farmers' fields since the 1700s. Stalks of grain are bent at their strongest points, the nodes. They may be bent in several different directions to make the flattened image in the field. The stalks are never broken, only bent. Some researchers say that the designs are too detailed and precise to have been done in the dark, but that is when crop circles appear to form.

Some circles are as big as football fields. Over 10,000 crop circles have been reported, and 90 percent of them appear in southern England. So far, crop circles have been found in 29 countries and have appeared in fields of wheat and barley.

? Why do you think crop circles are created on farmland?

Quick Fact
Crop circles generally form between two and four o'clock in the morning during the shortest evenings of the English year when darkness lasts only four hours.

THEORY #1

Some people believe crop circles cannot be made by humans because of the detail and intricate work. The patterns are very regular, and this suggests that they were made by a machine. Some people believe supernatural beings create these crop circles. The circles may be the marks left by a space craft or messages written by a high-energy beam from a UFO (unidentified flying object).

THEORY #2

Scientists, such as Dr. Colin Andrews, say that about 20 percent of crop circles are probably caused by eddies, circular movements in the Earth's magnetic field. Others are human-made. Besides, there's no proof that UFOs exist. In some cases, people have stepped forward and claimed responsibility for making crop circles. In a well-publicized case in 1998, the makers of a crop circle were caught by a large group of people. One reason that more people haven't been caught may be that crop circles are created at night.

? Some people have taken responsibility for crop circles when they haven't made them. Why do you think people come forward to take credit for something, even if they didn't do it?

The Expert Says...

" It is perfectly natural to ask if crop circles are hoaxes. But very difficult to explain why they cannot be hoaxed satisfactorily. "

—Pat Delgado, former NASA [National Aeronautics and Space Administration] engineer

CROP CIRCLE (LEFT)—COURTESY OF LUCY PRINGLE; CROP CIRCLE (RIGHT)—COURTESY STEVE ALEXANDER; OTHER IMAGES—SHUTTERSTOCK

CROP ART?

These bizarre creations are cropping up everywhere. Just check out these amazing profiles ...

This is an image of a crop circle in Alton Barnes, Wiltshire, England.

Cash Crop

In 1996, a crop circle was found in a field near the mysterious Stonehenge monument. Instead of complaining about his bad luck, one farmer had a great idea. He set up a booth and charged tourists a fee to see the circles. In four weeks he had collected $47,000. If the crop had been harvested, he would have earned $235!

Outside the Box

John Lundberg is an artist who started Circlemakers — a group of people who have made some pretty impressive crop circles. The members of Circlemakers don't just make crop circles to be sneaky, they do it to make money. They have created crop circles for movies, TV, music videos, advertisements, and PR stunts.

Lundberg also made an appearance on the TV show *Monster Garage* where he had to turn a tractor into a mechanical crop-circle maker.

> Does reading about John Lundberg convince you that crop circles are made by people? Why or why not?

Scary Movie

In the 2002 film *Signs*, writer and director M. Night Shyamalan insisted on using real crop circles instead of computer-generated ones. Mel Gibson stars as a farmer who wakes up one morning to find huge patterns carved into his crops. We won't give it away, but strange things start happening as he tries to find out the spooky source of the circles.

Quick Fact

One theory suggests that the water inside the plant stalks is rapidly boiled by a kind of microwave energy. Stalks can then be bent more easily by another energy source. Light, sound, and magnetic energies act together to form crop circles. What causes these energies to work together cannot be explained.

Take Note

Are crop circles human-made or created by supernatural beings? Will we ever know? Like Bigfoot, this mystery is intriguing. But unlike Bigfoot, crop circles have been seen by millions of people. That is why they are ranked #3.
- Do you think it's possible for people to create crop circles? Why or why not?

In this photo, Elvis is at the peak of his success. If he is still alive, he would be in his mid-70s.

LEY

ELVIS- PHOTO BY FOTOS INTL./KEYSTONE CANADA. (©) COPYRIGHT 2001 BY FOTOS INTL.

WHEN: Soon after his reported death on August 16, 1977

WHERE: All over the United States

SOMETHING STRANGE … Long live the King? Has Elvis really been living a secret life after faking his death in 1977, or is this just the wishful thinking of thousands of heartbroken fans?

For the last 30 years, people have seen Elvis sneaking into movie theaters, buying gas, and even playing bingo. Are these folks just seeing things, or is there really something to the rumors that Elvis Presley, the King of Rock and Roll, is still alive?

On August 16, 1977, the world was shocked when it was reported that Elvis had died of a drug overdose at the age of 42. During his career, Elvis had made a huge impact on the music, clothes, and films of the 1950s and 1960s. His millions of fans were saddened by the loss. Almost immediately after his death, the questions started — and so did the sightings. Why is Elvis's middle name spelled differently on his gravestone? Why did his coffin weigh over 880 pounds? At the time of his death, Elvis weighed 250 pounds. Why did several people at the funeral say the body looked nothing like him?

ELVIS PRESLEY

THE PLOT THICKENS

Those who believe that Elvis is still alive always mention the misspelling on his gravestone. Throughout his life, on all official documents, his middle name was spelled "Aron." But on the gravestone it is spelled "Aaron." If Elvis was really dead, wouldn't his father have corrected the error? When Elvis was born, his father went to a lot of trouble to change his birth certificate from "Aaron" to "Aron."

Quick Fact

Every year tens of thousands of fans recognize the day of Elvis's death by making a trip to his home in Memphis, Tennessee. There, they pay respects at his grave, celebrate his life, and participate in a candlelight vigil.

In 1970, Elvis met with President Richard Nixon at the White House. This is the most requested photo at the U.S. National Archives.

THEORY #1

Elvis felt like he was a prisoner of his own fame. He couldn't go out in public without being swarmed by fans, and he received many death threats. He was depressed about the direction his career had taken. Also, he had lost a lot of money in a shady business deal. Some people believe that he worked with the government to expose the crime ring that cheated him. For Elvis's protection, he faked his own death, and the government gave him a new identity.

THEORY #2

Throughout the world there are probably thousands of people who look like Elvis. Maybe the sightings are just fans who are unable to accept the fact that he is gone. Elvis changed the music scene and changed people's lives. More than 30 years after his death, he remains an important part of our culture. From 2001 to 2005, he was the top-earning dead celebrity. It is easy to see why people can't let go of him.

Quick Fact

Elvis Presley has had more than 149 songs on the Billboard Hot 100 Chart. He has been officially recognized by the Recording Industry Association of America as the bestselling solo artist in U.S. history.

Every year, Elvis's grave is visited by millions.

ELVIS
AARON
PRESLEY
JANUARY 8, 1935
AUGUST 16, 1977
SON OF
VERNON ELVIS PRESLEY
AND
GLADYS LOVE PRESLEY
FATHER OF
LISA MARIE PRESLEY
HE WAS A PRECIOUS GIFT FROM GOD
E CHERISHED AND LOVED DEARLY.

Living Dead?

Still not convinced about Elvis's state of being? Check out these facts that keep this strange mystery a hot topic for people to discuss.

Enough Said

In a press conference just after Elvis's death, his manager, Colonel Tom Parker, said, "Elvis didn't die. The body did. We're keeping up the good spirits. We're keeping Elvis alive. I talked to him this morning and he told me to 'carry on.'"

? These words could have a double meaning. What do you think Parker means?

Truth Be Told

Two days before his death, Elvis phoned a friend named Miss Foster. He told her that he wasn't going to go on his upcoming tour. She asked if he was ill, and he said no. He then told her that his troubles would soon be over, and that she shouldn't tell anyone. Miss Foster later took a lie-detector test, which suggested she was not lying about this incident.

Weight and See

In the weeks before his death, Elvis was supposed to go on an extensive concert tour. He didn't order any new costumes even though he had gained about 50 pounds since his last tour. It has been said that Elvis was embarrassed by the weight he had gained. Even though Elvis weighed about 250 pounds when he died, his death certificate lists him as weighing 170 pounds. This original certificate went missing, and the new one is dated two months after his "death."

Dead Weight

Some people say Elvis's coffin weighed over 880 pounds. They believe that this is because it held a wax version of Elvis that needed an air conditioner to keep it from melting. Weird? Absolutely!

Elvis plays a criminal-turned-superstar in the 1957 film Jailhouse Rock.

The Expert Says...

" Elvis Presley is a mystery that will never be solved. "

— Nick Tosches, music writer and biographer

Take Note

This mystery ranks #2. It has kept people fascinated for over 30 years. Elvis's impact on society was so powerful that he has not faded from people's memories. Some still want to believe that he is alive.

• Go online and check out the *Forbes* list of top-earning dead celebrities. Make a list of any qualities that these people have in common.

1 BERMUDA

There are extremely strong and violent winds in the Bermuda Triangle. It's rare to see a ship sinking in the Bermuda Triangle, but this image

TRIANGLE

WHEN: Evidence recorded from the days of Christopher Columbus in the late 15th century

WHERE: The three points of the Bermuda triangle are Bermuda; Miami, Florida; and San Juan, Puerto Rico.

SOMETHING STRANGE ... Ships and planes have vanished in this area, and wreckage and bodies are rarely found.

Have you thought about taking a trip to the Bermuda Triangle? You might want to think again! Many ships and planes have disappeared in this part of the Atlantic Ocean, including ones that belong to the U.S. military. They disappear without a trace and often without even sending out a distress signal.

For hundreds of years, pilots and ship captains traveling through the Bermuda Triangle have reported strange happenings. They see fire, unusual light, and floating ghost ships. They even smell rotten eggs!

Is there an explanation for these strange events? Not really, but there are many theories — from the ocean current, the environment, and the magnetic field in the area to aliens from outer space!

Many people will admit they are afraid of the Bermuda Triangle. Some will describe the fascination as silly. Whatever the case may be, ships and planes have gone missing and no one knows why.

BERMUDA TRIANGLE

THE PLOT THICKENS

The Bermuda Triangle is an area in the Atlantic Ocean that is shaped like, well, a triangle. The three points are Bermuda, Miami, and San Juan. In the last century, more than 50 ships and 20 planes have disappeared within the area, never to be seen or heard from again.

THEORY #1

Sailors and pilots regularly report magnetic changes in this area. Their compass needles do not work properly, and many of them lose their way. Could this be caused by star gates? Star gate is the name given to what some people believe is an opening or tunnel from our world to other dimensions in space and time. This is also an area where many claim to have seen UFOs.

THEORY #2

Some scientists believe there is a layer of methane deposits over the sea beds under the Bermuda Triangle. Under some conditions, the methane becomes unstable and changes into gas. When a pocket of methane gas explodes suddenly, it creates waterspouts like tornadoes. They will suck up anything in their paths — ships, boats, and even planes.

---

methane: *colorless, odorless flammable gas produced when organic matter breaks down*

? There are many stories that try to convince people that the Bermuda Triangle is dangerous. Do you sometimes make up stories to explain what you don't understand? How does this help?

Quick Fact

A number of mysterious disappearances have also occurred in an area off the east coast of Japan.

The Expert Says...

" Still, given a choice between ... an alien abduction versus human error ... and a temperamental Mother Nature — who could resist the legend of the Bermuda Triangle? "

— Hillary Mayell, *National Geographic News*

ALL IMAGES—SHUTTER

10   9   8   7   6

THE MYSTERY OF FLIGHT 19

On December 5, 1945, the mysterious circumstances of this U.S. Navy training mission took the lives of 27 men. Check out this timeline of the mission and decide whether the strange forces of the Bermuda Triangle are responsible …

2:10 PM Five torpedo bombers take off from the Naval Air Station in Fort Lauderdale, Florida. Flight 19 is a routine practice mission with Lieutenant Charles Taylor in charge.

2:45 PM Taylor sends a radio message indicating that his compasses are not working.

4:45 PM Communication is bad, but the base picks up a few words indicating Taylor is lost.

5:50 PM The base receives very weak signals. It cannot determine Taylor's location.

6:20 PM The bombers are low on fuel. The base sends boats to search for the bombers.

7:04 PM Flight 19 makes its last transmission. Planes search the area through the night and the next day. There is no sign of Flight 19.

Quick Fact

According to the U.S. Navy and Coast Guard, the high casualties in the Bermuda Triangle area could be due to heavy shipping and air traffic in the region.

So what happened to Flight 19? Many on the base believed the bombers ran out of fuel, ran into strong winds, and crashed into the cold waters. But why was there no wreckage?

The Bermuda Triangle is in an area of the Atlantic Ocean through which the Gulf Stream flows. There are often strong winds and violent, unexpected storms. Its stormy waters can easily swallow up distressed planes, leaving no sign of a disaster.

Flight 19 simply vanished. No one from the five planes were ever heard from or seen again.

Take Note

The Bermuda Triangle ranks #1. Like many of the previous mysteries, this one has remained unsolved for hundreds of years. Unlike the *Mary Celeste*, this one is not a single event. It has seemingly taken the lives of many people over time. It poses a threat even today.

• Read at least two other sources of information about the Bermuda Triangle. Record your findings on a chart with these headings: source, information, and fact or fiction. Then decide what you think is causing all of the disappearances in the Bermuda Triangle.

We Thought ...

Here are the criteria we used in ranking the 10 strangest mysteries.

The mystery:
- Puzzled the experts
- Included bizarre circumstances
- Occurred repeatedly over an extended period of time
- Has had an impact on life and property
- Was horrific or frightening
- Remains unsolved after a long time
- Has been witnessed by several credible sources
- Was suspected to be paranormal or supernatural
- Was dangerous or deadly

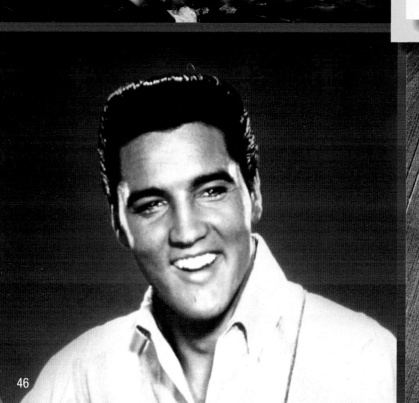

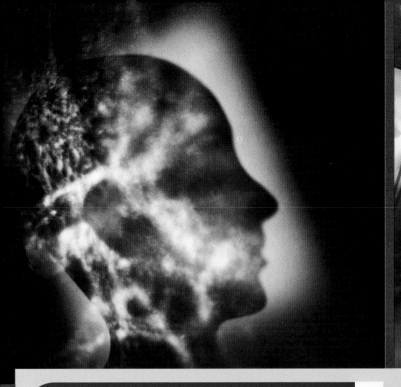

What Do You Think?

1. Do you agree with our ranking? If you don't, try ranking them yourself. Justify your ranking with data from your own research and reasoning. You may refer to our criteria, or you may want to draw up your own list of criteria.

2. Here are three other mysteries that we considered but in the end did not include in our top 10 list: Stonehenge, UFOs, and the city of Atlantis.
   - Find out more about them. Do you think they should have made our list? Give reasons for your response.
   - Are there other strange mysteries that you think should have made our list? Explain your choices.

Index

A

Andrews, Colin, 36
Apache, 11–13
Arizona, 11, 13
Arnold, Larry, 17
Atlantic Ocean, 23, 27–28, 43–45

B

Begg, Paul, 28
Bender, Frank, 9
Bermuda Triangle, 42–45
Bigfoot, 20, 30–33
Bleak House, 17
Boeing 727, 9
Bower, Dave, 36
Briggs, Captain Benjamin, 28–29

C

Canada, 29, 33
Calgary, 33
Chorley, Doug, 36
Columbus, Christopher, 43–44
Circlemakers, 37
Clarke, Arthur C., 16
Clarke, Bobby, 33
Coast Guard, 45
Cooper, D.B., 6–9
Cravey, James A., 13
Crop circles, 34–37
Crowley, Walt, 8
A Current Affair, 33

D

de Haan, Dr. John, 16
Dei Gratia, 28
Delgado, Pat, 36
Dickens, Charles, 17

E

Earhart, Amelia, 22–25
England, 21, 35-36

F

FBI, 8–9
Flight 19, 45

G

Genoa, 28
Gibraltar, 28
Gibson, Mel, 35, 37
Globe and Mail, The, 33
Grimlin, Bob, 32
Gulf Stream, 45

H

Holden, Henry M., 25
Howland Island, 23–24

J

Jailhouse Rock, 41
Japan, 24, 44

K

Kollenborn, Tom, 16

L

Lae, New Guinea, 23–24
Lindbergh, Charles, 22
Loch Ness Monster, 20
Lost Dutchman Mine, 10–13, 17
Lundberg, John, 37

M

Mary Celeste, 26–29, 45
Mayell, Hillary, 44
Memphis, 39–40
Methane, 17, 44
Miami, 24, 43–44
Moneymaker, Matt, 33
Monster Garage, 37
Mothman, 18–21, 33

N

Napier, John, 32
Native peoples, 31–32
Navy, 45
Nixon, Richard, 40
Noonan, Fred, 23–25
Nova Scotia, 29

O

Oregon, 7–8

P

Pacific Ocean, 23–24
Parker, Colonel Tom, 41
Patterson, Roger, 32
Miguel, Don, 11–13
Point Pleasant, 19–21
Portland 7–9
Presley, Elvis, 38–41
Puerto Rico, 43

R

Recording Industry Association of America, 40
Roosevelt, Franklin D., 24

S

San Juan, 44
Shyamalan, M. Night, 35, 37
Signs, 35, 37
Silver Bridge, 20
Spain, 27
Spontaneous Human Combustion, 14–17
Superstition Mountain, 10–13
Superstition Mountain Historical Society, 12

T

Taylor, Lietenant Charles, 45
Tennessee, 39–40
Tosches, Nick, 41

U

UFO, 44, 47
U.S. News, 9

V

Vasquez de Coronado, Francisco, 12–13

W

Walton, Dawn, 33
Waltz, Jacob, 11–13
Washington, 7
Weber, Duane, 9
Wilderness Hunter, The, 33
World War II, 24